BLUE DIAMOND

D0457538

The KidHaven Science Library

Thunderstorms

by Patricia D. Netzley

KIDHAVEN
PRESS™

THOMSON
———✦———™
GALE

San Diego • Detroit • New York • San Francisco • Cleveland
New Haven, Conn. • Waterville, Maine • London • Munich

THOMSON

GALE ™

© 2003 by KidHaven Press. KidHaven Press is an imprint of The Gale Group, Inc., a division of Thomson Learning, Inc.

KidHaven™ and Thomson Learning™ are trademarks used herein under license.

For more information, contact
KidHaven Press
27500 Drake Rd.
Farmington Hills, MI 48331-3535
Or you can visit our Internet site at http://www.gale.com

LIBRARY OF CONGRESS CATALOGING-IN-PUBLICATION DATA

Netzley, Patricia D.
    Thunderstorms / by Patricia D. Netzley.
      p. cm. — (The KidHaven science library)
Includes bibliographical references (p.).
Summary: Discusses thunderstorms, to include: development, rain, wind, thunder, lightning, tornadoes, forecasting, and monitoring.
    ISBN 0-7377-1017-9 (hardback : alk. paper)
    1. Thunderstorms—Juvenile literature. [1. Thunderstorms.] I. Title. II. Series.
    QC968.2 .N68 2003
    551.55'4—dc21

                                    2002009467

Printed in the United States of America

Contents

Chapter 1

How Thunderstorms Form

A thunderstorm is any storm accompanied by the booming sound of thunder. Such storms most often occur during the spring and summer, when they produce rain. They can also happen as part of a winter snowstorm. But no matter when they occur, all thunderstorms produce flashes of electricity called lightning, because thunder cannot exist without lightning. Other possible products of thunderstorms are hail, strong winds, and tornadoes.

In the United States, thunderstorms occur approximately one hundred days each year. Some parts of Africa and Indonesia have more than double that amount. Scientists estimate that there are more than 16 million thunderstorms throughout the world each year. A thunderstorm might last only a minute or it might last several hours. However, most thunderstorms last less than three hours, with the average being from ten to thirty minutes.

Hot and Cold Air

Thunderstorms start to form when masses of hot and cold air come together. These meetings between air masses can occur in two ways. In the first way, a series of small masses, or pockets, of air

A bolt of lightning shoots from a thundercloud, lit by the setting sun.

As a thunderstorm approaches, cold and warm air collide, creating a long flat cloud that looks like a shelf.

along the ground becomes hot. This is usually because the ground has been heated by summer sunshine, and the heat rises into the sky. (Whenever air is heated, it rises, because it then becomes lighter than the air above it.) If the pockets contain moisture, when they meet the cold air of the atmosphere they form clouds. If these clouds grow into the type that produce thunder, the air pockets become known as thunderstorm cells.

The second way that masses of cold and hot air come together is a result of air currents that move across Earth. These winds sometimes blow cold air masses into hot ones, or they blow hot air masses into cold ones. When a moving cold air mass hits an unmoving warm air mass, it creates a cold front. When a moving warm air mass hits an unmoving cold air mass, it creates a warm front. In either case, these fronts are places where the edge of a warm air mass is atop a cold air mass. If the warm air is also moist, as it rises over the cold air it forms clouds all along the front. This creates a frontal thunderstorm. If the front is very long (perhaps more than a thousand miles, or more than two hundred miles longer than California when the state is measured from north to south), several individual thunderstorms form in a line. Together this storm system is known as a line thunderstorm, or a squall.

Cloud Formation

The reason clouds form from moist, hot air is because of a process called **condensation**, by which **water vapor** leaves a mass of air. The amount of water vapor that air can hold depends on its temperature; warm air can hold more water vapor than cold air. Therefore when warm air comes into contact with cold air and begins to cool, it can no longer hold as much water vapor. As a result, the water vapor leaves, or condenses out of, the warm air as water droplets. The temperature level where condensation begins to occur is called the condensation level, or the dewpoint.

All clouds are formed because of condensation, but not all clouds produce rain or thunder. In fact, clouds fall into different categories depending on what they look like and how high in the atmosphere they have formed. For example, cirrus clouds are high-level clouds that look like wispy strands. (*Cirrus* is Latin for "lock of hair.") Because they form high up where the air is very cold, they are made of ice crystals instead of water droplets. Any rain they produce will usually **evaporate** before it reaches the ground.

In contrast, cumulus clouds are white, puffy clouds with a flat underside that look somewhat like a pile of snow. (*Cumulus* is Latin for "pile.")

Sometimes cumulus clouds develop into cumulonimbus clouds (seen here) that produce powerful thunderstorms.

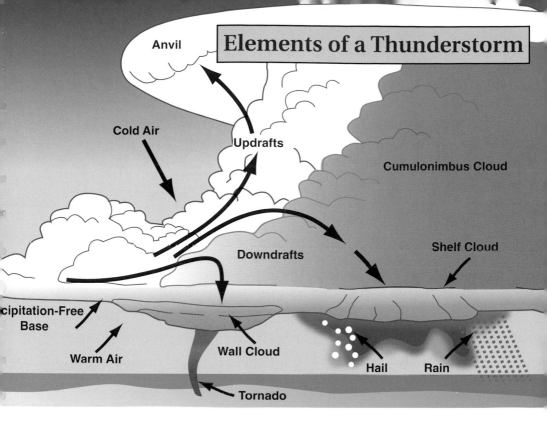

Their bases are at a low **altitude** (generally no higher than sixty-five hundred feet), and they can appear in the sky on warm spring or summer days. They do not usually produce rain. However, they can easily grow into the type of cloud that produces a thunderstorm: the cumulonimbus cloud, also known as a thundercloud or thunderhead. (*Nimbus* is Latin for "shower.")

The Growth of a Thundercloud

A cumulus cloud becomes a cumulonimbus cloud only when it grows to a height of about 20,000 feet or more, with the size depending on how cold the air around the developing cloud is. (By comparison, the 102-story Empire State Building in New York is only 1,250 feet tall.) A pocket of hot air continues to rise only until it cools down to the temperature of the air around it. And if the surrounding air is very cold, it takes longer for the temperature of the air pocket to match it. In addition, the colder the surrounding air, the faster the pocket of air rises, so that it does not even begin to cool until it has already reached a great height.

Meanwhile, water vapor in the rising air gives off heat as it condenses to form a cloud, helping the cloud maintain its warm temperature and grow bigger. In most cases, cloud growth is also fueled by warm air currents known as updrafts, which continue to rise from the ground as the cumulus cloud becomes a cumulonimbus cloud. The time during which this change from one type of cloud to another happens usually takes only ten to fifteen minutes. It is called the cumulus stage of a thunderstorm. Once the cumulus cloud has grown into a cumulonimbus cloud, the thunderstorm is in the mature stage. During this stage, the cumulonimbus cloud continues to grow taller and broader.

Cumulonimbus Clouds

Some cumulonimbus clouds are several miles wide and more than 70,000 feet tall (more than twice the height of Mount Everest in the Himalayas, which at 29,035 feet is the world's highest mountain). In the

Boaters stop to observe a towering thunderhead.

United States, most cumulonimbus clouds grow to be about 40,000 to 65,000 feet tall. Because of their great height, these clouds also have the coldest tops of all types of clouds. And the temperature difference between the top and the bottom of such clouds can be great. For example, some cumulonimbus clouds have a temperature of 100°F at their bottom and -100°F at their top.

The tallest cumulonimbus tops are flat, because they have reached the upper edge of a layer of Earth's atmosphere, the troposphere. In the tropo-

This billowing cumulonimbus cloud looks like a big puffy pillow in the sky.

sphere, the air is colder the higher up it is. But in the next highest level of the atmosphere, the stratosphere (around thirty to thirty-five miles above Earth), the air is warmer. This change in temperature, along with the intense energy the cloud has to use to reach the bottom of the stratosphere, makes the cloud top become flat and spread out.

In addition, the cloud top forms ice crystals because of the extreme cold at the upper edge of the troposphere. These ice crystals are then carried away by a system of powerful winds called the jet stream, which blows across Earth at high altitudes. The removal of the ice crystals often makes the flat top of the cloud appear to have been polished smooth.

Sometimes, however, a strong updraft will punch through this smooth top to give it a puffy area. Strong winds in the atmosphere might also break off parts of the cloud to form new ones of various types, but especially layers of cirrus clouds. Meanwhile, the cumulonimbus cloud continues to produce more water because of condensation. Eventually this water begins to fall to the ground as rain, hail, or snow.

Chapter 2

Precipitation and Winds

W hile cumulonimbus clouds are growing, their updrafts keep any water droplets and ice crystals that they are producing up in the sky. However, at a certain point the size of the cloud and the amount of its moisture become so large that the updrafts can no longer hold up these materials. As a result, the water and ice fall to the ground in the form of rain, snow, and hail, all of which are known as **precipitation**. Along with this precipitation comes much of the air from the lower part of the cloud, in the form of downward winds called downdrafts. Once near the ground, these downdrafts can create very strong horizontal gusts of wind.

Rain

The typical heavy thunderstorm produces one inch of rainfall. This means that about 3 million raindrops fall on every square yard of ground in the area of the cumulonimbus cloud. For every acre of land, this one inch of rainfall equals an amount of water weighing 226,000 pounds.

Some thunderstorms produce more than an inch of rainfall, sometimes in a very short amount of time. For example, in Unionville, Maryland, in July 1956, a one-minute thunderstorm produced 1.23 inches of rain. This storm holds the U.S. record for producing the most amount of rainfall per minute. The largest U.S. thunderstorm on record took place in Thrall, Texas, in September 1921. It produced 36.40 inches of rain during an eighteen-hour period.

Dark thunderclouds, heavy with rain, loom over these storm chasers in Nebraska.

Thunderstorms that produce a lot of rain in a short period of time can cause flash floods, which are floods that appear suddenly and unexpectedly. These floods can cause a great deal of damage. For example, in July 1976 a thunderstorm dropped about twelve inches of rain in one afternoon, right over the Big Thompson River near Fort Collins, Colorado. This amount of water swelled the river and produced floodwaters that headed downstream through Big Thompson Canyon. As the water entered the narrow canyon, the river grew so high that it swept away some of the thousands of people then camping beside the river. The flood also

Sheets of rain soak the soil as a thunderstorm passes over a plain in Wyoming.

destroyed many houses and businesses, as well as a major highway. When it was over, more than 139 people had died, and the amount of damage to property was more than $164 million.

Hail

Although most thunderstorms drop their moisture as rain, a few produce snow. When this happens, the amount of snowfall is large, usually three inches or more in an hour. Far more common than snow, however, is hail. A shower of ice balls, hail is produced only by spring and summer thunderstorms. (Some people call the frozen raindrops that fall from winter storms hail, too, but the correct word for this is sleet.)

Not all thunderstorms produce hail, however, and some areas are more likely to have hail than others. In the United States, for example, Florida thunderstorms rarely produce hail, while Wyoming and Colorado thunderstorms often do. Throughout the United States forty-eight hundred hail-producing thunderstorms occur each year.

An individual ball of hail, or a hailstone, can be as small as a pea or as large as a grapefruit. The largest hailstone on record, which fell in Canada, had a **diameter** of more than 17 inches and weighed almost 2 pounds. The biggest hailstone in the United States, which fell in Coffeyville, Kansas, on September 3, 1970, had a diameter of 5.7 inches and

A storm chaser finds a baseball-size hailstone.

Thunderstorms

weighed 27 ounces. (By comparison, a baseball is about 3 inches in diameter and weighs just over 5 ounces.) There have been reports in the country of Bangladesh of hailstones weighing more than 2 pounds, but none have been documented.

Hail usually falls from thunderstorm clouds in swaths, or lines. Most of these swaths are about 5 miles long and one-half mile wide. Some, however, get much larger. For example, one Illinois thunderstorm in 1968 produced a swath of hail 51 miles long and 19 miles wide, resulting in mounds of ice totaling 82 million cubic feet. Some thunderstorms have dropped enough hail to create individual mounds 6 feet high.

Like the floods that thunderstorms can produce, hail can cause serious damage to homes and businesses and even kill people and animals. For example, in 1986 a thunderstorm in China produced large hailstones that struck and killed about one hundred people and injured nine thousand. In July 1978 hail in Montana killed more than two hundred sheep. Throughout the United States, hail damages at least $1 billion worth of crops and property each year.

Severe Thunderstorms

If a thunderstorm produces hailstones that are bigger than three-fourths of an inch in diameter, it is classified as a severe thunderstorm. A thunderstorm is also

A swirling tornado sweeps across farmland in Montana.

have been clocked at 120 to 140 miles per hour. In some cases, thunderstorm winds can go from as little as 2 miles per hour to 80 miles per hour or more in less than a minute. This can quickly turn a thunderstorm from mild to severe without warning.

Downdrafts are also what cause a thunderstorm to end. As a storm progresses and its precipitation increases, its downdrafts gradually block the storm's updrafts. Without this supply of warm, moist air rising from the ground, the storm's clouds begin to shrink. During this period of cloud evaporation, called the dissipation stage, some large storm systems will lose clouds in some places only to develop new ones in others. Even a thunderstorm that appears to be ending can still cause serious damage.

Chapter 3

Thunder and Lightning

Whether a thunderstorm is severe or mild, by definition it produces thunder, and therefore it produces lightning as well. The two always occur together, even when people in the area of a storm do not see its lightning. In fact, more than 80 percent of all lightning occurs within one thundercloud (in which case it is known as in-cloud, or IC, lightning) or between one thundercloud and another (in which case it is called cloud-to-cloud, or CC, lightning), so high up in the sky that it is difficult or impossible to see.

Positive and Negative Charges

Lightning is a release, or discharge, of electricity caused by the energy within a thunderstorm system (or, on rare occasions, within clouds of gases produced by volcanoes). The process that triggers this discharge is so complicated that scientists do not fully understand it. Basically, though, the discharge is caused by the meeting of an area charged

Lightning shatters the night over Los Angeles.

Thunderstorms

with positive electrical energy with an area charged with negative electrical energy. For example, IC lightning is triggered by ice crystals at the top of the cloud, which are positively charged, coming into contact with water droplets at the bottom of the cloud, which are negatively charged.

Cloud-to-Ground Lightning

Similarly, lightning that travels from the cloud to the ground, also known as cloud-to-ground, or CG, lightning, is caused when the negative charge of the cloud's bottom meets with one or more areas of positive charge that develop on the ground beneath the cloud. Because opposite charges attract one another, a strand of electrical charge from within the cloud is drawn toward the positively charged ground at a speed of about two hundred thousand miles per hour. (At this speed, which is eleven times faster than a space shuttle, the charge would travel eight times around Earth in just one hour.) As the strand, which might be as thin as a pencil, emerges from the cloud, a similar strand from the ground comes up to meet it, connecting the charges and causing the bright flash of electricity.

The strand of electricity from within the cloud is called the leader; the strand from the ground is called the return stroke. When several return strokes come up to meet a leader from a series of positively charged ground areas, the result is a flash called forked lightning, because it looks like a fork pointed downward. The flash caused by a single return stroke and leader, which looks like a zigzagging line, is called a lightning bolt. Lightning that flickers is caused by many return strokes—sometimes forty or more—with each individual stroke lasting only a fraction of a second.

Electricity, Heat, and Sound

The amount of current, or flow, of electrical charge within each lightning discharge is equal to an average of thirty-thousand **amps**. However, some lightning discharges can be as little as a few thousand amps and others more than three hundred thousand. The **volts** in a lightning bolt can be as many as 20 million, producing as much light as more than 100 million lightbulbs.

Lightning also creates an amount of heat that is about five times greater than that of the sun. This intense heat—around 54,000°F—turns the air around the lightning into a gas called plasma, which reaches a temperature of about 18,000°F. The plasma's heat causes the air around the plasma to expand with great force and speed, disturbing the surrounding atmosphere with a series of high-pressure waves. This disturbance causes the booming sound of thunder.

Thunder can be as loud as 120 **decibels** (about ten times louder than a chainsaw). However, the sound of thunder does not usually travel very far from its source. In most cases it cannot be heard from more than ten miles away in an otherwise quiet countryside, or one to two miles away in a noisy city. In addition, because sound travels more slowly than light, a person who sees a flash of lightning does not hear its accompanying thunder until several seconds later. In fact, people can determine their distance from a lightning strike by counting the number of seconds between its flash of light and the sound of its thunder. This number divided by five equals the number of miles between the people and the lightning.

Deadly Strikes

According to some estimates, CG lightning occurs about 25 to 30 million times a year. As a result, the odds of a person being hit by a lightning bolt during

Lightning strikes in several places at the same time.

Lightning brightens the sky over Canada. Lightning kills more people each year than tornadoes or floods.

a year are around 1 in 300,000. In the United States, approximately 75 to 150 people are killed by lightning each year, which is more than the number killed as a result of tornadoes, hurricanes, and, in most years, floods. About 10 percent of the time, two deaths result from just one lightning strike, and about 1 percent of the time a strike causes three or more deaths.

However, about 70 percent of people who are struck by lightning survive their experience, although they often need medical help. For example, in 2001 professional golfer Michael Utley was playing on a golf course in Cape Cod, Massachusetts, when he was struck by lightning. The force of the electrical jolt was so strong that it blew off his shoes and stopped his heart. Paramedics revived him using CPR (cardiopulmonary resuscitation), a medical technique that restarts a heart that has stopped beating. Although he survived, he almost died again in the ambulance on the way to the hospital.

Most lightning-strike deaths occur because the lightning bolt has stopped the beat, or blood-pumping action, of the victim's heart. This action is regulated by natural electrical impulses within the heart that can be disrupted by jolts of electricity. The electricity of a strike can cause other health

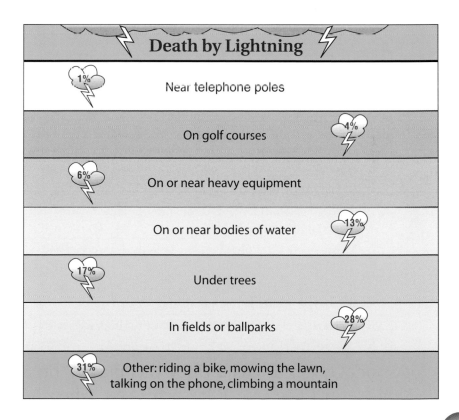

Death by Lightning

1%	Near telephone poles	
	On golf courses	4%
6%	On or near heavy equipment	
	On or near bodies of water	13%
17%	Under trees	
	In fields or ballparks	28%
31%	Other: riding a bike, mowing the lawn, talking on the phone, climbing a mountain	

problems as well, sometimes continuing long after the incident has passed. For example, victims can suffer skin burns, eardrum ruptures, brain damage, and/or problems with their nervous system and muscles. Many cannot remember what happened to them, even if they were conscious during the strike. This was the case with Utley, who has no memory of his lightning strike. He spent thirty-eight days in the hospital after the incident and then needed three months of physical therapy to be able to move properly again.

Lightning Facts and Fiction

fiction	Lightning never strikes the same place twice.
	Lightning has "favorite" sites that it may hit many times during one storm.
	If it is not raining there is no danger from lightning.
	Lightning often strikes outside of heavy rain and may occur as far as 10 miles away from rainfall.
facts	The rubber soles of your shoes or rubber tires will protect you from being struck by lightning.
	Rubber-soled shoes and rubber tires provide no protection from lightning.
	People struck by lightning carry an electrical charge and should not be touched.
	Lightning-strike victims carry no electrical charge and should be attended to immediately.
	"Heat lightning" occurs after very hot summer days and poses no threat.
	What is referred to as heat lightning is actually lightning from a thunderstorm too far away for thunder to be heard.

Risky Activities

Utley was at particular risk for being struck because of his profession. Statistics show that golfers, boaters, and other people who spend a lot of time outdoors near sources of water, such as a lake or tree (which holds moisture in its leaves), are at a higher risk of being struck by lightning. This is because water is an excellent conductor of electricity. Therefore, some golf courses have lightning detector alarms to warn golfers when electrical activity is nearby. Such an alarm sounded on the course where Utley was playing golf, just fifteen seconds before he was struck.

Statistics also show that living in certain locations increases the risk of being struck. For example, there is a higher risk of being struck in Florida, which in a typical year has as many as ninety thunderstorms. It also has the most CG lightning in the United States. People who live at high elevations or engage in mountain climbing are at a greater risk of being struck as well, because the forces that create lightning tend to occur at the highest points along the ground.

For the same reason, a man on horseback is at a greater risk of being struck than someone walking beside him, as long as nothing taller is nearby. The tallest object in any given area is the most likely to attract a lightning bolt during a thunderstorm. In fact, even just leaning against a tall object outdoors

The Empire State Building in New York City is struck by lightning several times each year.

is dangerous during a thunderstorm. This is because the electricity of a lightning strike can travel from the object into the person on its way to make the connection between the cloud and the ground. However, if the tallest object in an area is a poor conductor, or transmitter, of electricity, then something shorter will be struck instead.

Because they are good conductors of electricity, trees and towers are often struck by lightning. As a result, lightning strikes are a major cause of fires in national forests and routinely destroy power lines and other electrical equipment throughout the country. Certain tall buildings, such as the Empire State Building, are struck by lightning several times each year, sometimes causing disruption in their power as well.

Lightning is also a serious hazard for airline pilots because when a plane is struck by lightning, its electrical equipment can be damaged. Therefore, research is being done to protect planes from the effects of lightning. In addition, scientists are continually looking for better ways to predict where a thunderstorm might form, and then track such a storm's movements so that pilots can avoid flying into areas where lightning might strike.

Chapter 4

Forecasting and Monitoring Thunderstorms

B ecause thunderstorms are so dangerous, scientists have developed ways to predict when they might happen. They use modern technology to track the movement of thunderstorms and the air systems that create them. Scientists also routinely try to determine how large a developing thunderstorm might become. In addition, they study existing storm systems to improve their understanding of how the forces within thunderstorms work. From this research, they have learned that although thunderstorms can be deadly, they also play an important role in making Earth fit for human life.

The National Weather Service

Many government and public research facilities and universities study thunderstorms. But the most significant studies on thunderstorms in the United States are conducted at the National Severe Storms

Laboratory, run by the U.S. government in Norman, Oklahoma, with the involvement of the University of Oklahoma. Associated with this laboratory is the Storm Prediction Center, which issues thunderstorm and tornado warnings. These warnings enable people to take shelter in safe places whenever severe storms might be approaching.

The first government storm warning was issued in November 1870 by the U.S. Signal Corps, a government agency, in response to severe weather

Modern technology helps scientists forecast and monitor powerful thunderstorms.

over the Great Lakes. Earlier that year, the corps was placed in charge of a newly created national weather service. Initially called the U.S. Weather Service and later renamed the National Weather Service, in 1891 its management was transferred to the Department of Agriculture and in 1940 to the Department of Commerce.

It was not until 1953, however, that the service made its first tornado warning. Prior to this time, it was illegal for anyone in the United States to issue such a warning, because the government believed that people would panic upon hearing the warning and get hurt in their rush to escape the tornado. Only after several tornadoes occurred where an early warning would have saved lives did the government change its policy.

Satellites

The main way that U.S. scientists predict thunderstorms is through the use of weather **surveillance** satellites, the first of which were sent into space during the 1960s. About a half dozen such satellites orbit Earth over the equator at an altitude of 22,248 miles, while others travel over the North and South Poles. These satellites have special cameras that take pictures of Earth, usually every ten to fifteen minutes, so that scientists can study cloud patterns and movements.

In addition, the satellites have sensors, called sounders, that measure the **infrared radiation** (a

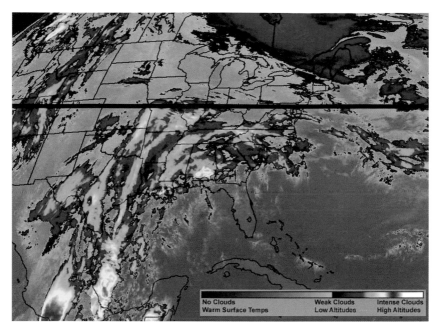

| No Clouds | | Weak Clouds | Intense Clouds |
| Warm Surface Temps | | Low Altitudes | High Altitudes |

Satellite images show the movement of severe weather around the world.

form of light that is invisible to the eye but still gives off heat) at various levels of the atmosphere. By measuring nineteen different wavelengths of this radiation using heat-sensing devices, scientists can determine atmospheric temperature and humidity. These measurements, called soundings, also provide information about various atmospheric gases, including water vapor.

Other types of soundings are made by using weather balloons released twice daily at hundreds of places throughout the world. The sounders of these balloons are a different form of technology from those in satellites, but their purpose is basically the same. As the balloons rise into the stratosphere, their

Researchers rely on measurements recorded by weather balloons to help them determine the strength and speed of an approaching storm.

sounders provide information about temperature and humidity, as well as about winds and air pressure. This allows scientists to track the movements of warm and cold fronts and determine where a thunderstorm might form. The information gathered can also help scientists determine how stable the atmosphere is, so they will know how severe a developing thunderstorm might become. However, whereas satellites relay their information back to Earth by computer, the readings from balloons are stored in little packages attached to parachutes, which fall to Earth after their balloons burst.

Radar

Radar is another important tool for making weather predictions. The word *radar* comes from parts of the phrase "radio detection and ranging," which refers to the fact that radar uses radio waves to detect objects and measure their range, or distance, in a particular direction, from the radar system. This system sends out the radio waves as pings, which return to the sender when they hit a distant object, thereby measuring how long they have taken to travel to the object and back again. Because radio waves are also reflected back from water droplets, ice crystals, and other matter within thunderstorms, radar is useful in tracking storm systems.

The type of radar used for modern weather tracking is called Doppler radar. Doppler uses computers

A radar antenna, seen propped on the nose of this airplane, warns pilots of hazardous weather conditions.

to show not only the location of an object and its distance from the radar system, but also its speed, direction of travel, and density, or solidity. The National Weather Service has a network of Doppler radar systems throughout the United States and is improving

This Doppler radar dish helps scientists monitor developing storms.

this system to increase the accuracy and speed of its weather forecasts.

The most advanced Doppler radar systems, called the NEXRAD (Next Generation Radar) systems, have improved the accuracy of tornado warnings from 30 percent to 80 percent in just a few years. These systems also provide a warning at least twenty minutes before a tornado hits, because they detect tornado winds forming high within clouds rather than on the ground. Wind speeds within existing tornadoes are sometimes measured by a system called sodar (sound detection and ranging). Sodar uses sound waves much like the radio waves of radar.

Models of Thunderstorms

The National Weather Service often uses computers to create models of developing thunderstorms. These models can help scientists figure out what geographical areas a particular storm might affect and what kind of precipitation and winds it might produce. Scientists have also used computer models to study a type of storm known as the supercell.

Although it is fed by only one thunderstorm cell (a rising pocket of warm air), a supercell thunderstorm is large and violent. In contrast, the ordinary single-cell thunderstorm is weak and small. The majority of large, violent thunderstorms are multicellular (that is, fed by many cells with clouds at different stages of development). Scientists do not

As technology advances, researchers will be able to monitor and forecast powerful thunderstorms more quickly and accurately.

fully understand why supercell thunderstorms are so much more powerful than ordinary single-cell thunderstorms. With computer models, however, scientists are gaining a greater understanding of how such storms and their tornadoes and lightning form.

The ultimate goal of such research is weather modification, whereby scientists attempt to lessen the force within thunderstorms to reduce the amount of weather-related damage. Specifically, scientists are trying to find ways to reduce wind speeds and stop tornadoes from forming. However, scientists do not wish to end thunderstorms altogether, because the storms' updrafts draw heat from the ground up into the atmosphere. Without this system for cooling the earth, some places would be at least 20°F hotter. This means that without thunderstorms, Earth would have more deserts and fewer places to live and grow crops.

altitude: The height above Earth's surface.

amps: Short for ampere, a unit for measuring current that is based on how much power is transferred from one place to another in one second.

condensation: The transformation of water from a gaseous form to a liquid.

decibels: Units used to express differences in power, usually related to acoustics (sound) or electric signals.

diameter: The length of a line passing from one side of a sphere to another, traveling through its center.

evaporate: To change into a vapor and become invisible to the eye.

infrared radiation: A type of light not visible to the eye but that gives off heat. For example, hot charcoal may not give off light, but it will give off infrared radiation.

precipitation: Moisture falling to Earth's surface as rain, snow, hail, sleet, etc.

surveillance: Close watch kept over something.

volts: Units representing the electrical potential and force between two ends of an electrical current.

water vapor: Droplets of moisture in the air that can barely be detected.

For Further Exploration

Books

Michael Allaby, *Guide to Weather: A Photographic Journey Through the Skies.* New York: Dorling Kindersley, 2000. This book uses photographs of weather phenomena to explain how weather works.

Rob Demillo, *How Weather Works.* Emeryville, CA: Ziff-Davis Press, 1994. For more advanced readers, this book provides detailed explanations, charts, and drawings related to various aspects of the weather.

Walter A. Lyons, *The Handy Weather Answer Book.* Canton, MI: Visible Ink Press, 1997. Written by a member of the American Meteorological Society, this book uses a question-and-answer format to offer many interesting facts and statistics related to the weather.

Websites

A-Z Weather Index (www.usatoday.com). Maintained by *USA Today,* this encyclopedic site allows people to look up weather topics alphabetically. It also provides current weather forecasts.

Dan's Wild Weather Page (www.wildweather.com). Answering weather questions for kids ages six to sixteen, this interactive weather page is maintained by meteorologist Dan Satterfield, who works for a news station in Huntsville, Alabama.

Index

Patricia D. Netzley is the author of dozens of books for children, young adults, and adults. Her nonfiction books include *The Stone Age, The Encyclopedia of Environmental Literature, The Curse of King Tut, Haunted Houses, Life on an Everest Expedition, The Encyclopedia of Women's Travel and Exploration, The Encyclopedia of Movie Special Effects,* and *The Encyclopedia of Witchcraft.*